An Alphabet of Obscure Feelings

Untranslatable Words (in Pictures)

Published by Doplin Books,
Brighton, UK
www.doplinbooks.com

ISBN: 9781798128480

To Apollo

A

Z

A

is for
Arbejdsglæde

Finding real satisfaction and

happiness in your work. (Danish)

B

is for
Boketto

Gazing vacantly into the distance,

without doing anything. (Japanese)

C

is for
Cavoli Riscaldati

An ill-advised attempt to revive an old

relationship. *Literally*: Reheated cabbage. (Italian)

is for
Dustceawung

Contemplating dust, in the knowledge

that it was once other people. (Old English)

is for

Estrenar

Wearing or using something for

the very first time. (Spanish)

F

is for
Firgun

Taking genuine pleasure in another

person's accomplishments. (Hebrew)

G

is for

Goya

When fantasy temporarily becomes

reality, thanks to good storytelling. (Urdu)

is for
Hiraeth

A longing for something from the past:

a home, an era, a person, a memory. (Welsh)

I

is for
Iktsuarpok

A feeling of anticipation before guests arrive, when

you can't stop checking to see if they're outside. (Inuit)

J

is for

Jeong

A connection that encompasses love, affection,

compassion, sharing, and community. (Korean)

is for
Kilig

The rush of romantic excitement you get

when you see the one you love. (Tagalog)

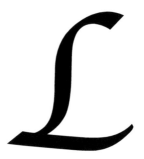

is for
L'appel du Vide

The urge to jump that you have to ignore

when you're standing in a high place. (French)

M

is for
Merak

Enjoying life's simple pleasures and

feeling at one with the universe. (Serbian)

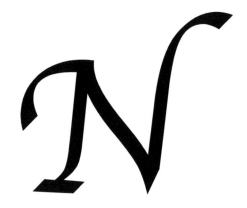

is for
Nachas

Taking pride in your child's achievements,

both the big and the small. (Yiddish)

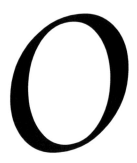

is for
Onsra

The bittersweet feeling that love won't last.

(Boro, India)

is for
Pono

A feeling of well-being and balance that comes

from living a good and righteous life. (Hawaiian)

Q
is for
Qingting

Listening very attentively with

alertness and courtesy. (Mandarin)

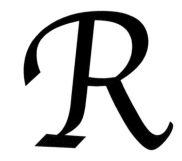

is for
Rasasvada

The taste of bliss in the absence of thought.

(Sanskrit)

S

is for
Saudade

Melancholic, nostalgic longing for

something or someone. (Portuguese)

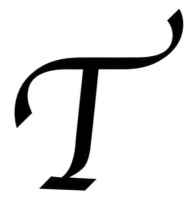

is for

Toska

A feeling of spiritual anguish

and deep ennui. (Russian)

is for
Ubuntu

The belief in a universal bond of sharing that

connects all humanity. (Nguni Bantu)

is for
Voorpret

Feeling pleasurable anticipation before an event.

Literally: Pre-fun. (Dutch)

is for
Waldeinsamkeit

The pleasant feeling of being alone in the woods.

(German)

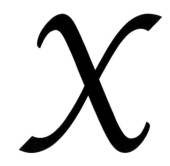

is for
Xenodochial

Feeling hospitable and friendly to strangers,

the opposite of xenophobic. (Greek)

Y

is for
Ya'aburnee

A love so deep, you hope to die before the person

you love does. *Literally*: You bury me. (Arabic)

Z

is for
Zooty

Flashy and ostentatious, extreme and flamboyant.

(American English)

A

Z

37985650R00035

Printed in Poland
by Amazon Fulfillment
Poland Sp. z o.o., Wrocław